Cultural Celebrations

RAMADAN

DiscoverRoo
An Imprint of Pop!
popbooksonline.com

Rachel Hamby

abdobooks.com

Published by Pop!, a division of ABDO, PO Box 398166,
Minneapolis, Minnesota 55439. Copyright © 2021 by POP, LLC.
International copyrights reserved in all countries. No part
of this book may be reproduced in any form without written
permission from the publisher. Pop!™ is a trademark and logo
of POP, LLC.

Printed in the United States of America, North Mankato,
Minnesota.

052020
092020

THIS BOOK CONTAINS
RECYCLED MATERIALS

Cover Photo: iStockphoto
Interior Photos: iStockphoto, 1, 5, 6, 9, 11, 12, 13, 14, 15, 17, 18, 19, 20,
21, 22 (bottom), 23 (top), 23 (bottom), 25, 26, 27, 28, 29, 30, 31;
Shutterstock Images, 7, 8, 22 (top)

Editor: Connor Stratton
Series Designer: Jake Slavik

Content Consultant: Suleyman Dost, PhD, Assistant Professor
of Classical Islam, Brandeis University

Library of Congress Control Number: 2019955004
Publisher's Cataloging-in-Publication Data

Names: Hamby, Rachel, author.
Title: Ramadan / by Rachel Hamby
Description: Minneapolis, Minnesota : POP!, 2021 | Series:
    Cultural celebrations | Includes online resources and
    index.
Identifiers: ISBN 9781532167720 (lib. bdg.) | ISBN 9781532168826
    (ebook)
Subjects: LCSH: Ramadan--Juvenile literature. | Holidays
    (Islamic law)--Juvenile literature. | Fasts and feasts--
    Islam--Juvenile literature. | Holidays--Juvenile literature.
    | Social customs--Juvenile literature.
Classification: DDC 297.3/62--dc23

WELCOME TO DiscoverRoo!

Pop open this book and you'll find QR codes loaded
with information, so you can learn even more!

Scan this code* and others like
it while you read, or visit the
website below to make this
book pop!

popbooksonline.com/ramadan

*Scanning QR codes requires a web-enabled smart device with a QR code reader app and a camera.

TABLE OF

CONTENTS

CHAPTER 1
A HOLY MONTH

A plate of dates sits on the table.

Meat dishes do too. It is the month of

Ramadan. The family has been fasting

all day. To fast is to go without food or

WATCH A
VIDEO HERE!

Families often have large feasts to break their Ramadan fasts.

drink. The sun finally sets. Everyone eats a

date to break the fast. Then they start the

meal. This meal is known as iftar.

A crescent moon shines over a mosque in Istanbul, Turkey.

Ramadan is a holy month for

Muslims. It begins on a different date

every year. This is because the Islamic

calendar follows the moon. Each month

begins with a **new moon**. Ramadan is the

ninth month of that calendar.

The sun sets at different times around the world. For this reason, iftar happens at different times around the world too.

DID YOU KNOW? The start date of Ramadan moves by 11 days every year. Over time, it passes through each season.

During Ramadan, Muslims do not eat or drink when the sun is up. They practice other **traditions** too. For example, people make extra efforts to be kind to others. They often give to **charity**.

During Ramadan, Muslims give food or money to the poor. This practice is called Zakat al-Fitr.

Some children receive gifts at the end of Ramadan.

CHAPTER 2
HISTORY OF RAMADAN

Islam is based on the teachings of
Muhammad. Muslims believe God spoke
to him in 610 CE. **Scribes** helped write
these words down. This writing became
Islam's holy book, the Quran.

LEARN MORE HERE!

The Quran is written in Arabic.

Muhammad was born in the city of Mecca. As a result, Islam teaches that this city is holy.

Muhammad lived in what is now

Saudi Arabia. Many people there followed

moon-based calendars. Muslims believe

Muhammad began receiving God's teachings during the month of Ramadan. So, that month became holy.

Muslims bow and face toward Mecca when they pray.

Ramadan lanterns are known as fanoos.

The Quran mentions fasting during

Ramadan. Other **traditions** formed over

the years. For example, people in Egypt

began making lanterns for Ramadan in

the 900s. These colored lights spread to

other countries over time.

DID YOU KNOW?

Today, Islam is the world's second-largest religion. There are more than one billion followers around the world.

Many Muslims gather to pray at their local mosque on Fridays.

CHAPTER 3

TRADITIONS

During Ramadan, Muslims focus on **self-control**. Fasting is one example. Fasting helps Muslims remember people in need. And it reminds them to be

COMPLETE AN ACTIVITY HERE!

thankful for what they have. Fasting can

also help people feel closer to God.

Ramadan is a time when Muslims give special focus to their faith.

Egg brik is a common suhoor food in Tunisia. This pastry holds egg, onion, tuna, harissa, and parsley.

But fasting is not the only **tradition**. Muslims also eat two meals during Ramadan. Suhoor is the meal before sunrise. After sunset, people eat iftar. Family and friends share this meal.

The foods they eat depend on their **culture**. In India, many people eat rice porridge. In Turkey, people often eat bread called pide.

Evening meals during Ramadan often include goat or lamb.

In some countries, each mosque's tall towers, called minarets, send out calls to prayer at set times of day.

During the year, traditional Muslims pray five times a day. During Ramadan, other prayers are added. Taraweeh is one of these prayers. For this prayer, Muslims read a different part of the Quran out loud each night.

By the end of Ramadan, people have often read the whole Quran during their Taraweeh prayers.

CELEBRATING RAMADAN

SUHOOR

Before sunrise, Muslims eat their first of two meals for the day. This meal tends to be healthy and balanced. It gives people energy to fast for the day.

FASTING

When the sun rises, people begin fasting. They don't eat or drink anything until the sun sets. Fasting can sometimes last 17 hours.

IFTAR

At sunset, people start eating their second meal of the day. Many break their fast with dates. Then they feast.

TARAWEEH

After dinner, Muslims often go to their mosque for prayer. This prayer involves reading parts of the Quran. It can sometimes last for two hours.

CHAPTER 4

EID AL-FITR

Ramadan ends when a **new moon** is seen. A group of religious leaders watch the sky. If they see a new moon, Ramadan is over. If not, the fasting lasts another day.

LEARN MORE HERE!

WAITING FOR THE NEW MOON

A new moon occurs when the moon is between Earth and the sun. It is difficult to see. Moon watchers look for a thin crescent moon at sunset.

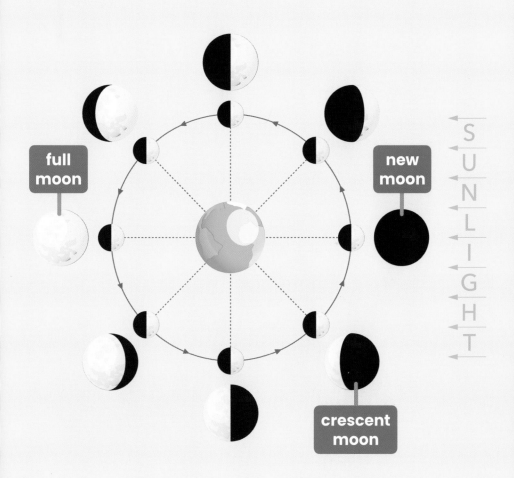

Muslims hold a festival at the end of Ramadan. The celebration is called Eid al-Fitr, or Eid. The festival lasts for three days. Eid begins with morning prayers. Many Muslims go to their mosque.

Thousands of people gather to pray at a mosque in India during Eid.

DID YOU KNOW?

Muslims often wear their best clothes for Eid. Muhammad also wore his best clothes for the festival.

ketupat

Ketupat are diamond-shaped rice cakes wrapped in leaves. They're often served on Eid, along with many side dishes.

Friends and families gather. They

eat a meal during the day. In Morocco,

warm flatbreads are eaten with mint tea.

In Turkey, people eat many treats and sweets. In India and Pakistan, people decorate their homes with lights.

Seviyan kheer is a sweet pudding made from noodles and milk. It's often topped with fruit and nuts.

MAKING CONNECTIONS

TEXT-TO-SELF

People eat many kinds of food during Eid. What is your favorite food to make or eat?

TEXT-TO-TEXT

Have you read books about other holidays that people celebrate? What do they have in common with Ramadan? How are they different?

TEXT-TO-WORLD

Fasting helps people practice self-control. What are some situations where having self-control is important?

GLOSSARY

charity – a place that collects money or things for people who are in need or suffering.

culture – the ideas, lifestyle, and traditions of a group of people.

new moon – a time when the sun and moon line up and the moon cannot be seen.

scribe – a person whose job is to copy text or speech.

self-control – the ability to not give in to what one wants or feels.

tradition – a belief or way of doing things that is passed down from person to person over time.

INDEX

ONLINE RESOURCES

popbooksonline.com

Scan this code* and others like it while you read, or visit the website below to make this book pop!

popbooksonline.com/ramadan

*Scanning QR codes requires a web-enabled smart device with a QR code reader app and a camera.